If found, kindly return to:

Name: _____

Phone: _____

Greatly appreciated

THE STRESS-LESS LIFE GUIDE
SUMMERTIME OR ANYTIME

TEENS

The simplest and most effective steps to a happier, healthier, and successful life!

CREATED BY
Dr. DIANNA M. and GABRIELLA K.
The Mother and Daughter Team

On top of our current monthly donations, a percentage of sales from ALL of our books will support children with mental and other health issues, some YouTube channels, and animal shelters which are helping abused and homeless animals.

Printed in the United States of America

First Printing, 2018

ISBN 978-1-7322971-3-5

Stress-Less Way Publishing

Connect with us:

Email: team@stresslessway.com

www.stresslessway.com

FOREWORD

Hello fellow readers! It is a privilege to introduce you to the world of The Stress-Less Life Guides. My name is Dr. Anton Fisher, D.O. I am a licensed and Board Certified Psychiatrist. I was asked to review the contents of these books. Having done so, I wholeheartedly recommend them to readers of all ages.

Stress, which is Anxiety by another name, has always been difficult to treat. There are various known forms of psychotherapy recommended for stress, and they often involve journaling. This series of guides will help lead you on a path of self-discovery and understanding of the underlying factors of what is causing your stress. Completing the exercises in the journals will be an outlet for your negative emotions and help to deflate your stressors from your day. Some of these guides are meant for children or adolescents. Completing them together with a parent will help create or strengthen your family bond. The guides can also be completed on your own, with family, or in conjunction with a professional therapist.

I personally know the authors of these guides and the circumstances that led them to want to help our society at large. Their combined wisdom, experience, and unique perspectives helped create these journals.

This series of guides will introduce you to some of those rare books that can be a benefit to everyone. I am confident that following the exercises in these journals will lead to a reduction in anxiety/stress levels and improved functioning at work, school, home, and life in general.

Dr. Anton Fisher, D.O.
Dr. Anton Fisher, D.O. is a Board Certified Psychiatrist practicing in multiple states, including Nevada. He is the founder of **TeleMind™**, a novel telepsychiatry clinic located in the Las Vegas Valley and beyond. More information can be found at www.telemindclinic.com.

*Disclaimer: I do not have a financial interest in these guides. These guides are not a substitute for medical advice. If you believe you are experiencing symptoms of a mood, anxiety, attention or other disorder, please consult with a mental health professional. I waive any liability for the content of these guides.

Disclaimer

Presented below, The Stress-Less Life Guide was created for educational and learning purposes only. Our ultimate goal is to provide a useful aid for anyone, including parents, professionals, schoolteachers and doctors. It is never too late to be on the way to your own Stress-Less life. Integrating our practices and methods into your lives on a daily basis will allow you and your loved ones to cope with stress more intelligently. You will learn how to guide yourself to a more fulfilling and stressless life. You will be in charge of your health, happiness, and future success. By following these Guides, you will be inspired to share your newfound skills with many others along your path.

OTHER GUIDES IN THIS SERIES:

- **THE STRESS-LESS LIFE GUIDE - TEENS.**
- **THE STRESS-LESS LIFE GUIDE - KIDS AND PARENTS.**
- **THE STRESS-LESS LIFE GUIDE - ADULTS.**
- **THE STRESS-LESS LIFE GUIDE - SUMMERTIME OR ANYTIME - KIDS AND PARENTS.**

ENJOY OUR:

NEWEST AND ONGOING SERIES OF INCREDIBLY INSPIRING STRESS-LESS COLORING BOOKS FOR DIFFERENT AGES.

These books include inspiring Quotes and Drawings from ACTUAL children and adults, some of whom have very challenging health issues.

WELCOME BACK!!!

HELLO AGAIN! WE MISSED YOU ALREADY!

THE MOTHER AND DAUGHTER TEAM IS HERE.
WE ARE THRILLED TO SEE YOU BACK!

THE VACATION IS FINALLY HERE!!!

THE GUIDE THAT YOU ARE HOLDING IN YOUR HANDS WILL HELP YOU TO STAY ON TRACK TO A HAPPY LIFE WITH LESS STRESS.

REMEMBER THE SAYING: **"PRACTICE MAKES PERFECT!"**

WE HOPE YOU WILL KEEP ENJOYING YOUR DAILY EXERCISES FROM THIS WORKBOOK.

YOU WILL DEFINITELY BE BETTER PREPARED TO DEAL WITH ANY PROBLEMS OR CONCERNS MORE INTELLIGENTLY THIS UPCOMING SCHOOL OR COLLEGE YEAR!

HAVE A HAPPY, HEALTHY, AND FUN VACATION, AND ENJOY YOUR FREE TIME!

LOVE AND PEACE

PRACTICE MAKES PERFECT

Steps to take daily or as needed:

The moment you feel stressed out or upset about something - **STOP:** BECOME MINDFUL AND AWARE. *Try to do the following:*

1. Limit your social media time to the minimum. Try to have a real face-to-face conversation with people you love and trust. Always remember YOU ARE NEVER ALONE with your problems and concerns! There is always someone around you who can help and guide you to proper solutions.

2. Tell yourself: "Tomorrow will be a better day, and my stress will be history. I am a healthy and happy individual." Even if you don't feel that way at that particular moment, make it as your mantra/affirmation. Repeat it as many times as needed to clear your mind from any negativity. Try to do it out loud if possible. That alone is a great way to start thinking positive thoughts.

3. Go to that positive place in your mind when you're stressed. Put as many happy thoughts and pictures as you want in that space and use them as needed. You can create your own inspirational quotes or use the ones from our Journal. You don't need many. *They have to be strong enough to serve as the switch from negative to positive.* That will be your own way out from your "stress bubble."

4. **Do what makes YOU happy:**
   - Listen to your favorite music.
   - Play your favorite instrument.
   - Spend time with positive people.
   - Read the books you love.
   - Watch a funny movie or video.
   - Just go outside for fresh air.
   - Draw.
   - Go to the Gym.

There is *no end* to fun stuff that you can do to direct your mind toward positive thinking.

5. On a daily basis, at your convenience - ideally, right before night time - write in this Journal the reason/reasons why you were stressed and what made your day better. *Share your thoughts with your family to get proper guidance and great ideas.*

IF NOTHING MADE YOU UPSET - **FANTASTIC!!!**
CONTINUE ENJOYING YOUR DAY AND WRITE DOWN ONLY WHAT MADE YOU HAPPY TODAY.

6. Give it some time (however much is needed - a day/two days/a week) and revisit that page later.

You will be in shock. Most of those problems you will not even remember. **Some** of those problems were out of your control to begin with, so why bother? **The rest** of them were solved one way or another, as always. Stressing out was for absolutely **NOTHING!!!**

THAT IS IT!!!
A simple and effective way to control your emotions and stress levels. It works for us every time. I am sure it will work for you as well.

BY BEING A MASTER OF YOUR OWN MIND, THOUGHTS, AND BEHAVIOR, **YOU AND ONLY YOU** WERE ABLE TO TURN A STRESSFUL DAY INTO A HAPPY DAY!

P.S. IN THE FUTURE, THESE GUIDES WILL BECOME PRICELESS MEMORIES AND LIFE LESSONS FOR YOU AND YOUR OWN CHILDREN - SAVE THEM!

LOVE AND PEACE

THE MOTHER AND DAUGHTER TEAM

DAILY JOURNAL

I AM SO THANKFUL AND READY FOR AN AMAZING NEW DAY.
CAN'T WAIT TO SEE WHAT IT WILL BRING TODAY!

Date ___/___/20__

STRESSFUL MOMENTS:

_____

_____

_____

HAPPY MOMENTS:

_____

_____

_____

PLAN AHEAD TODAY TO MINIMIZE YOUR STRESS TOMORROW.
(OR YOU CAN JUST WRITE OR DRAW SOMETHING SILLY DOWN BELOW AND GO TO
BED SMILING.)
PLANS FOR TOMORROW/TO DO LIST:

Date ___/___/20___

STRESSFUL MOMENTS:

_____

_____

_____

HAPPY MOMENTS:

_____

_____

_____

PLAN AHEAD TODAY TO MINIMIZE YOUR STRESS TOMORROW.
(OR YOU CAN JUST WRITE OR DRAW SOMETHING SILLY DOWN BELOW AND GO TO BED SMILING.)
PLANS FOR TOMORROW/TO DO LIST:

Date ___/___/20__

STRESSFUL MOMENTS:

_____

_____

_____

HAPPY MOMENTS:

_____

_____

_____

PLAN AHEAD TODAY TO MINIMIZE YOUR STRESS TOMORROW.
(OR YOU CAN JUST WRITE OR DRAW SOMETHING SILLY DOWN BELOW AND GO TO BED SMILING.)
PLANS FOR TOMORROW/TO DO LIST:

Date ___/___/20___

STRESSFUL MOMENTS:

_____

_____

_____

HAPPY MOMENTS:

_____

_____

_____

PLAN AHEAD TODAY TO MINIMIZE YOUR STRESS TOMORROW.
(OR YOU CAN JUST WRITE OR DRAW SOMETHING SILLY DOWN BELOW AND GO TO BED SMILING.)
PLANS FOR TOMORROW/TO DO LIST:

Date ___/___/20__

STRESSFUL MOMENTS:

_____

_____

_____

HAPPY MOMENTS:

_____

_____

_____

PLAN AHEAD TODAY TO MINIMIZE YOUR STRESS TOMORROW.
(OR YOU CAN JUST WRITE OR DRAW SOMETHING SILLY DOWN BELOW AND GO TO
BED SMILING.)
PLANS FOR TOMORROW/TO DO LIST:

Date ___/___/20___

STRESSFUL MOMENTS:

_____

_____

_____

HAPPY MOMENTS:

_____

_____

_____

PLAN AHEAD TODAY TO MINIMIZE YOUR STRESS TOMORROW.
(OR YOU CAN JUST WRITE OR DRAW SOMETHING SILLY DOWN BELOW AND GO TO
BED SMILING.)
PLANS FOR TOMORROW/TO DO LIST:

Date ___/___/20__

STRESSFUL MOMENTS:

_____

_____

_____

HAPPY MOMENTS:

_____

_____

_____

PLAN AHEAD TODAY TO MINIMIZE YOUR STRESS TOMORROW.
(OR YOU CAN JUST WRITE OR DRAW SOMETHING SILLY DOWN BELOW AND GO TO BED SMILING.)
PLANS FOR TOMORROW/TO DO LIST:

Date ___/___/20__

STRESSFUL MOMENTS:

_____

_____

_____

HAPPY MOMENTS:

_____

_____

_____

PLAN AHEAD TODAY TO MINIMIZE YOUR STRESS TOMORROW.
(OR YOU CAN JUST WRITE OR DRAW SOMETHING SILLY DOWN BELOW AND GO TO
BED SMILING.)
PLANS FOR TOMORROW/TO DO LIST:

Date ___/___/20__

STRESSFUL MOMENTS:

_____

_____

_____

HAPPY MOMENTS:

_____

_____

_____

PLAN AHEAD TODAY TO MINIMIZE YOUR STRESS TOMORROW.
(OR YOU CAN JUST WRITE OR DRAW SOMETHING SILLY DOWN BELOW AND GO TO
BED SMILING.)
PLANS FOR TOMORROW/TO DO LIST:

Date ___/___/20__

STRESSFUL MOMENTS:

_____

_____

_____

HAPPY MOMENTS:

_____

_____

_____

PLAN AHEAD TODAY TO MINIMIZE YOUR STRESS TOMORROW.
(OR YOU CAN JUST WRITE OR DRAW SOMETHING SILLY DOWN BELOW AND GO TO BED SMILING.)
PLANS FOR TOMORROW/TO DO LIST:

Date ___/___/20__

STRESSFUL MOMENTS:

_____

_____

_____

HAPPY MOMENTS:

_____

_____

_____

PLAN AHEAD TODAY TO MINIMIZE YOUR STRESS TOMORROW.
(OR YOU CAN JUST WRITE OR DRAW SOMETHING SILLY DOWN BELOW AND GO TO
BED SMILING.)
PLANS FOR TOMORROW/TO DO LIST:

Date ___/___/20__

STRESSFUL MOMENTS:

_____

_____

_____

HAPPY MOMENTS:

_____

_____

_____

PLAN AHEAD TODAY TO MINIMIZE YOUR STRESS TOMORROW.
(OR YOU CAN JUST WRITE OR DRAW SOMETHING SILLY DOWN BELOW AND GO TO BED SMILING.)
PLANS FOR TOMORROW/TO DO LIST:

Date ___/___/20__

STRESSFUL MOMENTS:

_____

_____

_____

HAPPY MOMENTS:

_____

_____

_____

PLAN AHEAD TODAY TO MINIMIZE YOUR STRESS TOMORROW.
(OR YOU CAN JUST WRITE OR DRAW SOMETHING SILLY DOWN BELOW AND GO TO BED SMILING.)
PLANS FOR TOMORROW/TO DO LIST:

Date ___/___/20__

STRESSFUL MOMENTS:

_____

_____

_____

HAPPY MOMENTS:

_____

_____

_____

PLAN AHEAD TODAY TO MINIMIZE YOUR STRESS TOMORROW.
(OR YOU CAN JUST WRITE OR DRAW SOMETHING SILLY DOWN BELOW AND GO TO BED SMILING.)
PLANS FOR TOMORROW/TO DO LIST:

Date ___/___/20__

STRESSFUL MOMENTS:

_____

_____

_____

HAPPY MOMENTS:

_____

_____

_____

PLAN AHEAD TODAY TO MINIMIZE YOUR STRESS TOMORROW.
(OR YOU CAN JUST WRITE OR DRAW SOMETHING SILLY DOWN BELOW AND GO TO BED SMILING.)
PLANS FOR TOMORROW/TO DO LIST:

Date ___/___/20__

STRESSFUL MOMENTS:

_____

_____

_____

HAPPY MOMENTS:

_____

_____

_____

PLAN AHEAD TODAY TO MINIMIZE YOUR STRESS TOMORROW.
(OR YOU CAN JUST WRITE OR DRAW SOMETHING SILLY DOWN BELOW AND GO TO BED SMILING.)
PLANS FOR TOMORROW/TO DO LIST:

Date ___/___/20__

STRESSFUL MOMENTS:

_____

_____

_____

HAPPY MOMENTS:

_____

_____

_____

PLAN AHEAD TODAY TO MINIMIZE YOUR STRESS TOMORROW.
(OR YOU CAN JUST WRITE OR DRAW SOMETHING SILLY DOWN BELOW AND GO TO
BED SMILING.)
PLANS FOR TOMORROW/TO DO LIST:

Date ___/___/20__

STRESSFUL MOMENTS:

_____

_____

_____

HAPPY MOMENTS:

_____

_____

_____

PLAN AHEAD TODAY TO MINIMIZE YOUR STRESS TOMORROW.
(OR YOU CAN JUST WRITE OR DRAW SOMETHING SILLY DOWN BELOW AND GO TO BED SMILING.)
PLANS FOR TOMORROW/TO DO LIST:

Date ___/___/20__

STRESSFUL MOMENTS:

_____

_____

_____

HAPPY MOMENTS:

_____

_____

_____

PLAN AHEAD TODAY TO MINIMIZE YOUR STRESS TOMORROW.
(OR YOU CAN JUST WRITE OR DRAW SOMETHING SILLY DOWN BELOW AND GO TO
BED SMILING.)
PLANS FOR TOMORROW/TO DO LIST:

Date ___ / ___ /20 __

STRESSFUL MOMENTS:

_____

_____

_____

HAPPY MOMENTS:

_____

_____

_____

PLAN AHEAD TODAY TO MINIMIZE YOUR STRESS TOMORROW.
(OR YOU CAN JUST WRITE OR DRAW SOMETHING SILLY DOWN BELOW AND GO TO BED SMILING.)
PLANS FOR TOMORROW/TO DO LIST:

Date ___/___/20__

STRESSFUL MOMENTS:

_____

_____

_____

HAPPY MOMENTS:

_____

_____

_____

PLAN AHEAD TODAY TO MINIMIZE YOUR STRESS TOMORROW.
(OR YOU CAN JUST WRITE OR DRAW SOMETHING SILLY DOWN BELOW AND GO TO BED SMILING.)
PLANS FOR TOMORROW/TO DO LIST:

Date ___/___/20___

STRESSFUL MOMENTS:

_____

_____

_____

HAPPY MOMENTS:

_____

_____

_____

PLAN AHEAD TODAY TO MINIMIZE YOUR STRESS TOMORROW.
(OR YOU CAN JUST WRITE OR DRAW SOMETHING SILLY DOWN BELOW AND GO TO BED SMILING.)
PLANS FOR TOMORROW/TO DO LIST:

Date ___/___/20___

STRESSFUL MOMENTS:

_____

_____

_____

HAPPY MOMENTS:

_____

_____

_____

PLAN AHEAD TODAY TO MINIMIZE YOUR STRESS TOMORROW.
(OR YOU CAN JUST WRITE OR DRAW SOMETHING SILLY DOWN BELOW AND GO TO BED SMILING.)
PLANS FOR TOMORROW/TO DO LIST:

Date ___/___/20__

STRESSFUL MOMENTS:

_____

_____

_____

HAPPY MOMENTS:

_____

_____

_____

PLAN AHEAD TODAY TO MINIMIZE YOUR STRESS TOMORROW.
(OR YOU CAN JUST WRITE OR DRAW SOMETHING SILLY DOWN BELOW AND GO TO
BED SMILING.)
PLANS FOR TOMORROW/TO DO LIST:

Date ___/___/20__

STRESSFUL MOMENTS:

_____

_____

_____

HAPPY MOMENTS:

_____

_____

_____

PLAN AHEAD TODAY TO MINIMIZE YOUR STRESS TOMORROW.
(OR YOU CAN JUST WRITE OR DRAW SOMETHING SILLY DOWN BELOW AND GO TO
BED SMILING.)
PLANS FOR TOMORROW/TO DO LIST:

Date ___/___/20__

STRESSFUL MOMENTS:

_____

_____

_____

HAPPY MOMENTS:

_____

_____

_____

PLAN AHEAD TODAY TO MINIMIZE YOUR STRESS TOMORROW.
(OR YOU CAN JUST WRITE OR DRAW SOMETHING SILLY DOWN BELOW AND GO TO BED SMILING.)
PLANS FOR TOMORROW/TO DO LIST:

Date ___/___/20__

STRESSFUL MOMENTS:

_____

_____

_____

HAPPY MOMENTS:

_____

_____

_____

PLAN AHEAD TODAY TO MINIMIZE YOUR STRESS TOMORROW.
(OR YOU CAN JUST WRITE OR DRAW SOMETHING SILLY DOWN BELOW AND GO TO BED SMILING.)
PLANS FOR TOMORROW/TO DO LIST:

Date ___/___/20__

STRESSFUL MOMENTS:

_____

_____

_____

HAPPY MOMENTS:

_____

_____

_____

PLAN AHEAD TODAY TO MINIMIZE YOUR STRESS TOMORROW.
(OR YOU CAN JUST WRITE OR DRAW SOMETHING SILLY DOWN BELOW AND GO TO
BED SMILING.)
PLANS FOR TOMORROW/TO DO LIST:

Date ___/___/20__

STRESSFUL MOMENTS:

_____

_____

_____

HAPPY MOMENTS:

_____

_____

_____

PLAN AHEAD TODAY TO MINIMIZE YOUR STRESS TOMORROW.
(OR YOU CAN JUST WRITE OR DRAW SOMETHING SILLY DOWN BELOW AND GO TO BED SMILING.)
PLANS FOR TOMORROW/TO DO LIST:

Date ___/___/20__

STRESSFUL MOMENTS:

_____

_____

_____

HAPPY MOMENTS:

_____

_____

_____

PLAN AHEAD TODAY TO MINIMIZE YOUR STRESS TOMORROW.
(OR YOU CAN JUST WRITE OR DRAW SOMETHING SILLY DOWN BELOW AND GO TO BED SMILING.)
PLANS FOR TOMORROW/TO DO LIST:

Date ___/___/20__

STRESSFUL MOMENTS:

_____

_____

_____

HAPPY MOMENTS:

_____

_____

_____

PLAN AHEAD TODAY TO MINIMIZE YOUR STRESS TOMORROW.
(OR YOU CAN JUST WRITE OR DRAW SOMETHING SILLY DOWN BELOW AND GO TO
BED SMILING.)
PLANS FOR TOMORROW/TO DO LIST:

Date ___/___/20__

STRESSFUL MOMENTS:

_____

_____

_____

HAPPY MOMENTS:

_____

_____

_____

PLAN AHEAD TODAY TO MINIMIZE YOUR STRESS TOMORROW.
(OR YOU CAN JUST WRITE OR DRAW SOMETHING SILLY DOWN BELOW AND GO TO BED SMILING.)
PLANS FOR TOMORROW/TO DO LIST:

Date ___/___/20___

STRESSFUL MOMENTS:

_____

_____

_____

HAPPY MOMENTS:

_____

_____

_____

PLAN AHEAD TODAY TO MINIMIZE YOUR STRESS TOMORROW.
(OR YOU CAN JUST WRITE OR DRAW SOMETHING SILLY DOWN BELOW AND GO TO
BED SMILING.)
PLANS FOR TOMORROW/TO DO LIST:

Date ___/___/20__

STRESSFUL MOMENTS:

_____

_____

_____

HAPPY MOMENTS:

_____

_____

_____

PLAN AHEAD TODAY TO MINIMIZE YOUR STRESS TOMORROW.
(OR YOU CAN JUST WRITE OR DRAW SOMETHING SILLY DOWN BELOW AND GO TO BED SMILING.)
PLANS FOR TOMORROW/TO DO LIST:

Date ___/___/20__

STRESSFUL MOMENTS:

_____

_____

_____

HAPPY MOMENTS:

_____

_____

_____

PLAN AHEAD TODAY TO MINIMIZE YOUR STRESS TOMORROW.
(OR YOU CAN JUST WRITE OR DRAW SOMETHING SILLY DOWN BELOW AND GO TO
BED SMILING.)
PLANS FOR TOMORROW/TO DO LIST:

Date ___/___/20__

STRESSFUL MOMENTS:

_____

_____

_____

HAPPY MOMENTS:

_____

_____

_____

PLAN AHEAD TODAY TO MINIMIZE YOUR STRESS TOMORROW.
(OR YOU CAN JUST WRITE OR DRAW SOMETHING SILLY DOWN BELOW AND GO TO BED SMILING.)
PLANS FOR TOMORROW/TO DO LIST:

Date ___/___/20__

STRESSFUL MOMENTS:

_____

_____

_____

HAPPY MOMENTS:

_____

_____

_____

PLAN AHEAD TODAY TO MINIMIZE YOUR STRESS TOMORROW.
(OR YOU CAN JUST WRITE OR DRAW SOMETHING SILLY DOWN BELOW AND GO TO
BED SMILING.)
PLANS FOR TOMORROW/TO DO LIST:

Date ___/___/20__

STRESSFUL MOMENTS:

_____

_____

_____

HAPPY MOMENTS:

_____

_____

_____

PLAN AHEAD TODAY TO MINIMIZE YOUR STRESS TOMORROW.
(OR YOU CAN JUST WRITE OR DRAW SOMETHING SILLY DOWN BELOW AND GO TO BED SMILING.)
PLANS FOR TOMORROW/TO DO LIST:

Date ___/___/20__

STRESSFUL MOMENTS:

_____

_____

_____

HAPPY MOMENTS:

_____

_____

_____

PLAN AHEAD TODAY TO MINIMIZE YOUR STRESS TOMORROW.
(OR YOU CAN JUST WRITE OR DRAW SOMETHING SILLY DOWN BELOW AND GO TO BED SMILING.)
PLANS FOR TOMORROW/TO DO LIST:

Date ___/___/20__

STRESSFUL MOMENTS:

_____

_____

_____

HAPPY MOMENTS:

_____

_____

_____

PLAN AHEAD TODAY TO MINIMIZE YOUR STRESS TOMORROW.
(OR YOU CAN JUST WRITE OR DRAW SOMETHING SILLY DOWN BELOW AND GO TO BED SMILING.)
PLANS FOR TOMORROW/TO DO LIST:

Date ___/___/20__

STRESSFUL MOMENTS:

_____

_____

_____

HAPPY MOMENTS:

_____

_____

_____

PLAN AHEAD TODAY TO MINIMIZE YOUR STRESS TOMORROW.
(OR YOU CAN JUST WRITE OR DRAW SOMETHING SILLY DOWN BELOW AND GO TO
BED SMILING.)
PLANS FOR TOMORROW/TO DO LIST:

Date ___/___/20__

STRESSFUL MOMENTS:

_____

_____

_____

HAPPY MOMENTS:

_____

_____

_____

PLAN AHEAD TODAY TO MINIMIZE YOUR STRESS TOMORROW.
(OR YOU CAN JUST WRITE OR DRAW SOMETHING SILLY DOWN BELOW AND GO TO BED SMILING.)
PLANS FOR TOMORROW/TO DO LIST:

Date ___/___/20__

STRESSFUL MOMENTS:

_____

_____

_____

HAPPY MOMENTS:

_____

_____

_____

PLAN AHEAD TODAY TO MINIMIZE YOUR STRESS TOMORROW.
(OR YOU CAN JUST WRITE OR DRAW SOMETHING SILLY DOWN BELOW AND GO TO BED SMILING.)
PLANS FOR TOMORROW/TO DO LIST:

Date ___/___/20__

STRESSFUL MOMENTS:

_____

_____

_____

HAPPY MOMENTS:

_____

_____

_____

PLAN AHEAD TODAY TO MINIMIZE YOUR STRESS TOMORROW.
(OR YOU CAN JUST WRITE OR DRAW SOMETHING SILLY DOWN BELOW AND GO TO
BED SMILING.)
PLANS FOR TOMORROW/TO DO LIST:

Date ___/___/20__

STRESSFUL MOMENTS:

_____

_____

_____

HAPPY MOMENTS:

_____

_____

_____

PLAN AHEAD TODAY TO MINIMIZE YOUR STRESS TOMORROW.
(OR YOU CAN JUST WRITE OR DRAW SOMETHING SILLY DOWN BELOW AND GO TO
BED SMILING.)
PLANS FOR TOMORROW/TO DO LIST:

Date ___/___/20__

STRESSFUL MOMENTS:

_____

_____

_____

HAPPY MOMENTS:

_____

_____

_____

PLAN AHEAD TODAY TO MINIMIZE YOUR STRESS TOMORROW.
(OR YOU CAN JUST WRITE OR DRAW SOMETHING SILLY DOWN BELOW AND GO TO
BED SMILING.)
PLANS FOR TOMORROW/TO DO LIST:

Date ___/___/20__

STRESSFUL MOMENTS:

_____

_____

_____

HAPPY MOMENTS:

_____

_____

_____

PLAN AHEAD TODAY TO MINIMIZE YOUR STRESS TOMORROW.
(OR YOU CAN JUST WRITE OR DRAW SOMETHING SILLY DOWN BELOW AND GO TO
BED SMILING.)
PLANS FOR TOMORROW/TO DO LIST:

Date ___ / ___ /20__

STRESSFUL MOMENTS:

_____

_____

_____

HAPPY MOMENTS:

_____

_____

_____

PLAN AHEAD TODAY TO MINIMIZE YOUR STRESS TOMORROW.
(OR YOU CAN JUST WRITE OR DRAW SOMETHING SILLY DOWN BELOW AND GO TO
BED SMILING.)
PLANS FOR TOMORROW/TO DO LIST:

Date ___/___/20__

STRESSFUL MOMENTS:

_____

_____

_____

HAPPY MOMENTS:

_____

_____

_____

PLAN AHEAD TODAY TO MINIMIZE YOUR STRESS TOMORROW.
(OR YOU CAN JUST WRITE OR DRAW SOMETHING SILLY DOWN BELOW AND GO TO BED SMILING.)
PLANS FOR TOMORROW/TO DO LIST:

Date ___/___/20__

STRESSFUL MOMENTS:

_____

_____

_____

HAPPY MOMENTS:

_____

_____

_____

PLAN AHEAD TODAY TO MINIMIZE YOUR STRESS TOMORROW.
(OR YOU CAN JUST WRITE OR DRAW SOMETHING SILLY DOWN BELOW AND GO TO BED SMILING.)
PLANS FOR TOMORROW/TO DO LIST:

Date ___/___/20__

STRESSFUL MOMENTS:

_____

_____

_____

HAPPY MOMENTS:

_____

_____

_____

PLAN AHEAD TODAY TO MINIMIZE YOUR STRESS TOMORROW.
(OR YOU CAN JUST WRITE OR DRAW SOMETHING SILLY DOWN BELOW AND GO TO
BED SMILING.)
PLANS FOR TOMORROW/TO DO LIST:

Date ___/___/20__

STRESSFUL MOMENTS:

_____

_____

_____

HAPPY MOMENTS:

_____

_____

_____

PLAN AHEAD TODAY TO MINIMIZE YOUR STRESS TOMORROW.
(OR YOU CAN JUST WRITE OR DRAW SOMETHING SILLY DOWN BELOW AND GO TO
BED SMILING.)
PLANS FOR TOMORROW/TO DO LIST:

Date ___/___/20__

STRESSFUL MOMENTS:

_____

_____

_____

HAPPY MOMENTS:

_____

_____

_____

PLAN AHEAD TODAY TO MINIMIZE YOUR STRESS TOMORROW.
(OR YOU CAN JUST WRITE OR DRAW SOMETHING SILLY DOWN BELOW AND GO TO
BED SMILING.)
PLANS FOR TOMORROW/TO DO LIST:

Date ___/___/20__

STRESSFUL MOMENTS:

_____

_____

_____

HAPPY MOMENTS:

_____

_____

_____

PLAN AHEAD TODAY TO MINIMIZE YOUR STRESS TOMORROW.
(OR YOU CAN JUST WRITE OR DRAW SOMETHING SILLY DOWN BELOW AND GO TO BED SMILING.)
PLANS FOR TOMORROW/TO DO LIST:

Date ___/___/20__

STRESSFUL MOMENTS:

_____

_____

_____

HAPPY MOMENTS:

_____

_____

_____

PLAN AHEAD TODAY TO MINIMIZE YOUR STRESS TOMORROW.
(OR YOU CAN JUST WRITE OR DRAW SOMETHING SILLY DOWN BELOW AND GO TO BED SMILING.)
PLANS FOR TOMORROW/TO DO LIST:

Date ___/___/20__

STRESSFUL MOMENTS:

_____

_____

_____

HAPPY MOMENTS:

_____

_____

_____

PLAN AHEAD TODAY TO MINIMIZE YOUR STRESS TOMORROW.
(OR YOU CAN JUST WRITE OR DRAW SOMETHING SILLY DOWN BELOW AND GO TO BED SMILING.)
PLANS FOR TOMORROW/TO DO LIST:

Date ___/___/20__

STRESSFUL MOMENTS:

_____

_____

_____

HAPPY MOMENTS:

_____

_____

_____

PLAN AHEAD TODAY TO MINIMIZE YOUR STRESS TOMORROW.
(OR YOU CAN JUST WRITE OR DRAW SOMETHING SILLY DOWN BELOW AND GO TO
BED SMILING.)
PLANS FOR TOMORROW/TO DO LIST:

Date ___/___/20___

STRESSFUL MOMENTS:

_____

_____

_____

HAPPY MOMENTS:

_____

_____

_____

PLAN AHEAD TODAY TO MINIMIZE YOUR STRESS TOMORROW.
(OR YOU CAN JUST WRITE OR DRAW SOMETHING SILLY DOWN BELOW AND GO TO BED SMILING.)
PLANS FOR TOMORROW/TO DO LIST:

Date ___/___/20__

STRESSFUL MOMENTS:

_____

_____

_____

HAPPY MOMENTS:

_____

_____

_____

PLAN AHEAD TODAY TO MINIMIZE YOUR STRESS TOMORROW.
(OR YOU CAN JUST WRITE OR DRAW SOMETHING SILLY DOWN BELOW AND GO TO BED SMILING.)
PLANS FOR TOMORROW/TO DO LIST:

Date ___/___/20__

STRESSFUL MOMENTS:

_____

_____

_____

HAPPY MOMENTS:

_____

_____

_____

PLAN AHEAD TODAY TO MINIMIZE YOUR STRESS TOMORROW.
(OR YOU CAN JUST WRITE OR DRAW SOMETHING SILLY DOWN BELOW AND GO TO
BED SMILING.)
PLANS FOR TOMORROW/TO DO LIST:

Date ___/___/20__

STRESSFUL MOMENTS:

_____

_____

_____

HAPPY MOMENTS:

_____

_____

_____

PLAN AHEAD TODAY TO MINIMIZE YOUR STRESS TOMORROW.

(OR YOU CAN JUST WRITE OR DRAW SOMETHING SILLY DOWN BELOW AND GO TO BED SMILING.)

PLANS FOR TOMORROW/TO DO LIST:

Date ___/___/20___

STRESSFUL MOMENTS:

_____

_____

_____

HAPPY MOMENTS:

_____

_____

_____

PLAN AHEAD TODAY TO MINIMIZE YOUR STRESS TOMORROW.
(OR YOU CAN JUST WRITE OR DRAW SOMETHING SILLY DOWN BELOW AND GO TO BED SMILING.)
PLANS FOR TOMORROW/TO DO LIST:

Date ___/___/20__

STRESSFUL MOMENTS:

_____

_____

_____

HAPPY MOMENTS:

_____

_____

_____

PLAN AHEAD TODAY TO MINIMIZE YOUR STRESS TOMORROW.
(OR YOU CAN JUST WRITE OR DRAW SOMETHING SILLY DOWN BELOW AND GO TO BED SMILING.)
PLANS FOR TOMORROW/TO DO LIST:

Date ___/___/20__

STRESSFUL MOMENTS:

_____

_____

_____

HAPPY MOMENTS:

_____

_____

_____

PLAN AHEAD TODAY TO MINIMIZE YOUR STRESS TOMORROW.
(OR YOU CAN JUST WRITE OR DRAW SOMETHING SILLY DOWN BELOW AND GO TO BED SMILING.)
PLANS FOR TOMORROW/TO DO LIST:

Date ___/___/20__

STRESSFUL MOMENTS:

_____

_____

_____

HAPPY MOMENTS:

_____

_____

_____

PLAN AHEAD TODAY TO MINIMIZE YOUR STRESS TOMORROW.
(OR YOU CAN JUST WRITE OR DRAW SOMETHING SILLY DOWN BELOW AND GO TO BED SMILING.)
PLANS FOR TOMORROW/TO DO LIST:

Date ___/___/20__

STRESSFUL MOMENTS:

_____

_____

_____

HAPPY MOMENTS:

_____

_____

_____

PLAN AHEAD TODAY TO MINIMIZE YOUR STRESS TOMORROW.
(OR YOU CAN JUST WRITE OR DRAW SOMETHING SILLY DOWN BELOW AND GO TO BED SMILING.)
PLANS FOR TOMORROW/TO DO LIST:

Date ___/___/20__

STRESSFUL MOMENTS:

_____

_____

_____

HAPPY MOMENTS:

_____

_____

_____

PLAN AHEAD TODAY TO MINIMIZE YOUR STRESS TOMORROW.
(OR YOU CAN JUST WRITE OR DRAW SOMETHING SILLY DOWN BELOW AND GO TO
BED SMILING.)
PLANS FOR TOMORROW/TO DO LIST:

Date ___/___/20__

STRESSFUL MOMENTS:

_____

_____

_____

HAPPY MOMENTS:

_____

_____

_____

PLAN AHEAD TODAY TO MINIMIZE YOUR STRESS TOMORROW.
(OR YOU CAN JUST WRITE OR DRAW SOMETHING SILLY DOWN BELOW AND GO TO BED SMILING.)
PLANS FOR TOMORROW/TO DO LIST:

Date ___/___/20__

STRESSFUL MOMENTS:

_____

_____

_____

HAPPY MOMENTS:

_____

_____

_____

PLAN AHEAD TODAY TO MINIMIZE YOUR STRESS TOMORROW.
(OR YOU CAN JUST WRITE OR DRAW SOMETHING SILLY DOWN BELOW AND GO TO
BED SMILING.)
PLANS FOR TOMORROW/TO DO LIST:

Date ___/___/20__

STRESSFUL MOMENTS:

_____

_____

_____

HAPPY MOMENTS:

_____

_____

_____

PLAN AHEAD TODAY TO MINIMIZE YOUR STRESS TOMORROW.
(OR YOU CAN JUST WRITE OR DRAW SOMETHING SILLY DOWN BELOW AND GO TO
BED SMILING.)
PLANS FOR TOMORROW/TO DO LIST:

Date ___/___/20__

STRESSFUL MOMENTS:

_____

_____

_____

HAPPY MOMENTS:

_____

_____

_____

PLAN AHEAD TODAY TO MINIMIZE YOUR STRESS TOMORROW.
(OR YOU CAN JUST WRITE OR DRAW SOMETHING SILLY DOWN BELOW AND GO TO BED SMILING.)
PLANS FOR TOMORROW/TO DO LIST:

Date ___/___/20__

STRESSFUL MOMENTS:

_____

_____

_____

HAPPY MOMENTS:

_____

_____

_____

PLAN AHEAD TODAY TO MINIMIZE YOUR STRESS TOMORROW.

(OR YOU CAN JUST WRITE OR DRAW SOMETHING SILLY DOWN BELOW AND GO TO BED SMILING.)

PLANS FOR TOMORROW/TO DO LIST:

Date ___/___/20__

STRESSFUL MOMENTS:

_____

_____

_____

HAPPY MOMENTS:

_____

_____

_____

PLAN AHEAD TODAY TO MINIMIZE YOUR STRESS TOMORROW.
(OR YOU CAN JUST WRITE OR DRAW SOMETHING SILLY DOWN BELOW AND GO TO BED SMILING.)
PLANS FOR TOMORROW/TO DO LIST:

Date ___/___/20__

STRESSFUL MOMENTS:

_____

_____

_____

HAPPY MOMENTS:

_____

_____

_____

PLAN AHEAD TODAY TO MINIMIZE YOUR STRESS TOMORROW.
(OR YOU CAN JUST WRITE OR DRAW SOMETHING SILLY DOWN BELOW AND GO TO BED SMILING.)
PLANS FOR TOMORROW/TO DO LIST:

Date ___/___/20___

STRESSFUL MOMENTS:

_____

_____

_____

HAPPY MOMENTS:

_____

_____

_____

PLAN AHEAD TODAY TO MINIMIZE YOUR STRESS TOMORROW.
(OR YOU CAN JUST WRITE OR DRAW SOMETHING SILLY DOWN BELOW AND GO TO
BED SMILING.)
PLANS FOR TOMORROW/TO DO LIST:

Date ___/___/20__

STRESSFUL MOMENTS:

_____

_____

_____

HAPPY MOMENTS:

_____

_____

_____

PLAN AHEAD TODAY TO MINIMIZE YOUR STRESS TOMORROW.
(OR YOU CAN JUST WRITE OR DRAW SOMETHING SILLY DOWN BELOW AND GO TO BED SMILING.)
PLANS FOR TOMORROW/TO DO LIST:

Date ___/___/20__

STRESSFUL MOMENTS:

_____

_____

_____

HAPPY MOMENTS:

_____

_____

_____

PLAN AHEAD TODAY TO MINIMIZE YOUR STRESS TOMORROW.
(OR YOU CAN JUST WRITE OR DRAW SOMETHING SILLY DOWN BELOW AND GO TO
BED SMILING.)
PLANS FOR TOMORROW/TO DO LIST:

Date ___/___/20__

STRESSFUL MOMENTS:

_____

_____

_____

HAPPY MOMENTS:

_____

_____

_____

PLAN AHEAD TODAY TO MINIMIZE YOUR STRESS TOMORROW.

(OR YOU CAN JUST WRITE OR DRAW SOMETHING SILLY DOWN BELOW AND GO TO BED SMILING.)

PLANS FOR TOMORROW/TO DO LIST:

Date ___/___/20__

STRESSFUL MOMENTS:

_____

_____

_____

HAPPY MOMENTS:

_____

_____

_____

PLAN AHEAD TODAY TO MINIMIZE YOUR STRESS TOMORROW.
(OR YOU CAN JUST WRITE OR DRAW SOMETHING SILLY DOWN BELOW AND GO TO
BED SMILING.)
PLANS FOR TOMORROW/TO DO LIST:

Date ___/___/20__

STRESSFUL MOMENTS:

_____

_____

_____

HAPPY MOMENTS:

_____

_____

_____

PLAN AHEAD TODAY TO MINIMIZE YOUR STRESS TOMORROW.
(OR YOU CAN JUST WRITE OR DRAW SOMETHING SILLY DOWN BELOW AND GO TO BED SMILING.)
PLANS FOR TOMORROW/TO DO LIST:

Date ___/___/20__

STRESSFUL MOMENTS:

_____

_____

_____

HAPPY MOMENTS:

_____

_____

_____

PLAN AHEAD TODAY TO MINIMIZE YOUR STRESS TOMORROW.
(OR YOU CAN JUST WRITE OR DRAW SOMETHING SILLY DOWN BELOW AND GO TO BED SMILING.)
PLANS FOR TOMORROW/TO DO LIST:

Date ___/___/20___

STRESSFUL MOMENTS:

_____

_____

_____

HAPPY MOMENTS:

_____

_____

_____

PLAN AHEAD TODAY TO MINIMIZE YOUR STRESS TOMORROW.
(OR YOU CAN JUST WRITE OR DRAW SOMETHING SILLY DOWN BELOW AND GO TO BED SMILING.)
PLANS FOR TOMORROW/TO DO LIST:

The MOTHER AND DAUGHTER TEAM would like to thank YOU again for a wonderful VACATION spent with us and we wish YOU all the luck and happiness for the upcoming school year!!!

LOVE AND PEACE

www.ingramcontent.com/pod-product-compliance
Lightning Source LLC
Chambersburg PA
CBHW081659270326
41933CB00017B/3226

9 781732 297135